Teenage Information Series

# The Healthy Body Book

Andrina E. McCormack

Chambers

Published by W & R Chambers Ltd, Edinburgh 1986

**British Library Cataloguing in Publication Data**

McCormack, Andrina E.
    The healthy body book.—(Teenage
    information series)
    1. Youth—Health and hygiene
    I. Title   II. Series
    613'.024055     RA564.5

ISBN 0 550 20565 9
ISBN 0 550 75218 8 Student ed.

Illustrations by Hazel McGlashan

Printing and Binding by Eyre & Spottiswoode Ltd, London and Margate

Teenage Health Care Series

The Healthy Body Book

**The Healthy Body Book**
Andrina E. McCormack, formerly educationist with the Scottish
Health Education Group, is now working full-time in education.

# Contents

# 1. Introduction

Health is something that many young people take for granted. When you are growing up it may be difficult to accept that what you are doing now will affect your health when you are 40, 50 or 60.

But you are laying the foundations of your health now, and you will have to rely on these foundations for many years to come.

If you start thinking about your health in your teens, then you learn to accept a healthy way of life naturally. In a way it becomes a habit.

The Healthy Body Book lays out the major areas of health which you should think about. It includes information on diet, exercise, hygiene and feeling good about yourself.

# 2. Healthy Inside

Food and our eating habits are important in many ways. Food helps us stay fit and well, and provides us with the essential nutrients we need if our bodies are to continue growing and remain healthy. People who do not eat properly become ill, and often someone going off his or her food is an early sign of illness. Eating is important socially to most people, but most of all, eating should be enjoyable.

## Eating and health

Food is necessary for our bodies to stay healthy, to replace old cells which die, and to develop new cells which help us grow. The food we eat can be put into different categories, and it is vital that we eat some things from each category, since different foods have different benefits. *Proteins* come from meat, fish and poultry, pulses, and from dairy products such as milk and cheese. Our bodies need protein to grow, especially during adolescence. *Minerals* include iron and potassium and come mainly from green vegetables such as cabbage, broccoli and brussels sprouts. Meat is rich in iron. We need minerals to maintain the healthy day-to-day working of our bodies. *Vitamins* come from fruit and vegetables and help build healthy cells. We generally take in enough vitamins every day with a normal diet, so there is no point in taking expensive multivitamin pills, especially as the body cannot store vitamins. When we have enough, our bodies get rid of the surplus. *Carbohydrates* are important to give us energy, and come from potatoes and bread. *Fats* help us burn up energy, but can be harmful to health if taken in too large amounts. It is better to eat low-fat foods such as yoghurt and cottage cheese rather than chips and fries. Finally, *fibre* is also vital for the health of our digestive and excretory systems. We need 'roughage' to help our bowels get rid of the waste products in our bodies. There is plenty of fibre in wholemeal and bran bread, cereals, peas and beans, and many fruit and vegetables.

You should regard these categories only as guidelines to the things different foods can do for you. Every type of food offers two or three benefits. For instance a baked potato gives you carbohydrates for energy, but it also gives you fibre and vitamins too. You should eat food you like and enjoy, but make sure that you eat food from all the categories. Today, there is a high level of heart disease which is increasing all the time and which is associated with our high intake of fats, sugar and salt. Many people still eat fried or fatty foods or dishes with rich sauces. You will still see a lot of people putting salt on their food before they have even tasted it. Too much fat and salt in your teens and early twenties can store up quite a bit of trouble for you later, but you should also think about what your diet is doing to you now. If you have spots for instance it may be because you are taking too much fat or sugar.

You probably have your meals cooked for you by your mother, father or houseparent. These meals will probably give you all the nutrients you need to stay healthy, but the snacks you eat between meals may not be doing you much good. Count the number of bags of crisps or bars of chocolate you eat, and remember, you can always say 'no'. Try to think of ways in which you can improve your diet.

Chrissie and her brother David both take lunch boxes to school. They each make up their own lunch at night to save their mother time in the morning. They used to eat white-bread sandwiches with cheese, and a packet of crisps. After reading 'The Healthy Body Book', they decided to try an experiment. Chrissie began to use wholemeal bread for her sandwiches and David started to use bran rolls because he has a bigger appetite than Chrissie. Instead of crisps, they both take fruit now. Chrissie's spots have cleared up considerably, and David does not get as hungry by two o'clock as he used to.

Food is also an important factor in the health of your teeth. Sugar in sweets and soft drinks makes your teeth decay and rot, but you can still enjoy snacks between meals if you really feel too hungry to wait. Foods which will not harm your teeth include nuts, fruit, vegetables and cereals. Try taking a small bag of rice crispies or cornflakes to school to nibble instead of sweets.

People all over the world eat lots of different things to stay healthy. There are probably many foods which you have heard of but never tasted. People are now able to travel to different countries all over the world, so there are more and more opportunities to taste food from the Far East, from China, and from many European countries.

Many people are *vegetarian,* which means they do not eat meat. If you look at a vegetarian cookery book, you will find that many recipes use pulses — lentils, peas and beans — as the basis for different dishes. A vegetarian diet is just as healthy as a diet which includes meat. Some people do not eat red meat (beef, mince, steak, etc.) but only eat what is known as white meat, things like chicken and fish. On the whole these are easier to digest. Some vegetarians eat eggs and cheese, but others do not eat anything from animals, and eat only naturally-grown foods. These people are called 'vegans'. Of course it is also possible to eat vegetarian food without giving up meat altogether.

Joe for example is 16 and is in training for the next Commonwealth Games. He is very interested in how his diet affects his training. He decided he would like to try some vegetarian meals to see the effects on his health, and because he does not really like meat all that much. He likes cooking and finds it easy to experiment because he comes home late after training, when the rest of the family have already eaten. However, he still eats what the rest of the family are having when they all eat together.

## Eating and illness

When you are not too well, one of the first signs you may notice is that you do not feel like eating. So you can see, there is a relationship — perhaps not always a very good one — between food and illness.

Another aspect of this relationship is the way your emotions can effect the way you eat. You may eat chocolate or sweets when you feel upset or depressed, or, if you are excited about a school trip, you may not want to eat anything. Once in a while, eating 'for comfort' or not eating at all will do you no harm.

A few young people, especially girls, go to extremes, sometimes eating too much or sometimes refusing to eat altogether. Many teenage girls worry that they are too fat and cut down on their food to lose weight. Most of them, however, are not too fat at all and should not worry. About one in a hundred becomes obsessed with losing weight and develops a condition called 'slimmer's disease'. The correct name for this is *anorexia nervosa*.

When a girl is anorexic, she becomes afraid that even the smallest amount of food will turn into fat. Even though she may be very skinny indeed, when she looks in the mirror she sees herself as being really fat. When a girl is suffering from *bulimia,* she eats huge quantities of food and then makes herself sick. Both these conditions are very serious indeed and need treatment from a doctor and other agencies which can help. These diseases can last a very long time, and are both complex and difficult to get over.

## Sociable eating

Happily, the majority of young people enjoy their food, and eating can be important as a social event. Some families eat together once a day and this gives them the chance to talk about what they have all been doing. Many people celebrate important events by going out for a meal, or eating something special with friends and relatives.

Food can be quite significant in a relationship between a boy and a girl, like the gift of a special box of chocolates on your birthday. Food also plays a large part in many religious ceremonies, and is an important part of a nation's history and culture.

*What We Say About Food*
The fact that food and eating play such a big part in our day-to-day lives is often found in the way we describe our feelings.

We say … 'I'm really fed up'

        … 'My stomach turned over'

        … 'That really stuck in my throat'

        … 'She looked good enough to eat'

Can you think of any other examples?

# 3. Healthy Outside

A lot of people think that health is just about being fit and taking exercise. That is only part of being healthy — but it is a very important part. Exercise helps the hundreds of muscles in your body to stay firm and stretchy. The more you use your muscles, the healthier they become. As you exercise, your heart pumps the blood faster, making all the different parts of your body, including your skin, feel healthier and more alive.

## Exercise

Most teenagers can get plenty of exercise in school during PE or games periods, and at home. Think of all the ways you exercise your body and keep fit.

Robin has spina bifida, so he cannot walk and has always been in a wheelchair. He has to keep his arm and upper-body muscles in top condition so that he can move his chair about himself. At school, Robin was a keen swimmer, because he could move around more easily in the water. Robin stays fit by sailing. He learned to sail three years ago in the Water Sports Centre in the country park near where he lives. Strength and fitness mean that Robin can be more and more independent as he grows up.

*The 'Three S' Rule*
There are three 'S's to consider when you are choosing which exercises are best and most enjoyable. Rowing, cycling, swimming, running and skiing are all good for

*Stamina,* or endurance. All these plus weightlifting are good for *Strength.* Swimming, yoga, aerobics and dance exercise all encourage *Suppleness.* You must choose an exercise that will help you improve each of your 'S' factors. Lots of other exercises are good for Strength, Stamina and Suppleness. Work out whether the way you exercise improves all three.

## Clothes

When you are taking part in any kind of exercise, it is important to wear the right kind of clothing. Tight-fitting clothes can restrict your movement and may cut into your skin or make it difficult to breathe. When you exercise you should sweat. Tight clothes may prevent you sweating properly because they soak up the perspiration and keep it close against your skin. Clothes which are suitable for exercise do not have to be expensive or 'special' in any way. You may already have some which are fine, so you may not have to buy more. Choose clothes which are loose and comfortable, and which will not get in your way or hamper your movements. Watch out too that you will not trip up on trousers that are too long, or get clothes that are too loose caught in equipment.

The right footwear is also important for exercising. Jogging or running with hard shoes can damage your knee and ankle joints, and shoes which do not give you support can set up problems with your back. If it is possible, you can do your feet a lot of good by exercising barefoot. But take care that there is no risk of stepping on something which may cut you. If you have a skin infection, or athlete's foot or verrucas do not go swimming as these infections are passed at swimming pools. Wear plastic shoes and take extra care too in the shower, so that you do not pass your infection to other people.

## Choosing an exercise

There are so many different sports to choose from that it can be difficult to decide. Try lots of different sports before you buy any equipment yourself, and choose something you enjoy doing — there is no point doing something you hate just because it is supposed to do you good. Fitness must be fun as well.

Some people complain that exercise and sport are too expensive. But there are lots of ways to take exercise outside without spending any money at all.

Tommy is into punk clothes and hairstyles, and spends a lot of time and money working on his motorbike. He lives in the centre of a large and very busy city, but likes to get away from all the noise and petrol smells to the park near his home. He hates running, but really enjoys walking round the park because he feels more relaxed in the fresh air, and it does not cost him a penny.

Most towns have at least one swimming pool and a sports centre which you can join and use as much as you like. Find out which pool or sports centre is nearest to your home and go along and try it, even just once.

As your body develops and changes in your teens, exercise is important to help you build up strength and energy. As well as the physical changes which your body goes through, you have to adjust mentally to being an adult. Some teenagers often feel quite depressed or low for no apparent reason, but exercise and taking part in something can help you get over this too. It may seem to be a huge effort to get started but it is worth it in the end.

Girls are sometimes told that they should not do any exercise, especially swimming, while they are having a period. Exercise can, in fact, help any cramps or pain, especially exercises which tone up the abdominal and pelvic muscles. You may need to change your sanitary pads more often, since you may bleed slightly faster. There is no need to be embarrassed or shy about doing any kind of sport while you are menstruating. Sanitary towels or tampons are small and discreet, so nobody need know if you do not want them to.

Exercise and sport should make you breathe faster, and cause you to sweat. So after exercising you should always shower or wash so that the perspiration does not lie on your skin and go stale. You do not need expensive sports talc or deodorant. Soap and water will clean your skin and help you feel fresh and alive.

# 4. Healthy on the Surface

Keeping clean and taking care of your body is not something you do only after exercising. Personal hygiene is an everyday matter, and care of hair, nails and skin is not just for girls. Both boys and girls have to take responsibility for looking after themselves.

13

Some people like to take a bath every day, but it is not always possible for a family to have endless hot water on tap. A shower uses only a fraction of the water you use in a bath. It can be a lot quicker and cheaper too.

Garry for instance has a quick shower every morning because he feels it wakes him up before he goes to school. His older sister Marie feels that the steam in a shower makes her hair go limp, so she prefers to have a body wash using the handbasin in the morning. Then she enjoys a lazy relaxing bath in the evening.

You can still keep thoroughly clean by washing in a basin. Every day you should make sure that you wash your underarms, your genital area, and any other sweaty restricted areas of your body. You can even give your feet a quick wash by sticking one foot at a time under the tap.

Human beings, like many other animals, wash their skin to take away the dust and grime that come from the air, and to wash away all the impurities which have come out through the skin, and with sweat. If you leave all this on your skin, you soon notice that people are avoiding you, because you smell of stale sweat and bad body odour, which is very unpleasant. Your skin too starts to complain, and produces spots and pimples to make sure that you take extra care.

Your body is changing and developing through your teens, so you may find that some of your body systems go out of balance. This is often most noticeable in skin, and most teenagers have to cope with spots and pimples which appear on their chins and round their noses. Spots can be controlled to a certain extent by watching what you eat. When they are caused by excess oil in your skin, you may want to try some of the medicated wash lotions that are for sale in chemists. These can be expensive, however, and may not be as successful as all the advertisements claim. When you put these on your skin, always use cotton wool and not tissues or paper hankies as many of these are quite rough and may harm your skin. Before you spend a huge amount on these special preparations, try something simple and straightforward, like regular washing with ordinary soap and water.

If you are very prone to spots ...

> ... do not use a highly perfumed soap as this may irritate your skin

> ... check your diet carefully for too much sugar, chocolate or fat

> ... watch that you do not spread infection by touching a spot and then touching another part of your face

> ... above all, do not pick or squeeze your spots, do not stick pins into them, and do not make them bleed as this can all cause permanent scarring

If you feel very uncomfortable or embarrassed about your skin, there are one or two other things you can try. After you have washed and dried your face, dab on a little distilled witch hazel, which you can buy very cheaply from the chemist. Witch hazel is made from the bark of certain trees, and is a gentle and light natural antiseptic which tones your skin and keeps it clean. Boys can use it too. Nobody needs to know you are using it because it is colourless and has no smell. Treating your skin to a steam bath can help it too. There are expensive facial saunas on the market, but a mixing bowl or handbasin and a thick towel are all you need. Pour a little boiling water into the bowl, cover your head with the towel and sit with your face over the water. The towel will trap the steam as it comes off the water. The heat may catch your breath, so make sure you can still breathe comfortably. If you drop a pinch of dried mint into the water you may find it relaxing to breathe the nice smell. Take care that you do not bend so close that you dip your nose in the water, and make sure that you put the bowl firmly on a table, where it will not be tipped over. After five or ten minutes, rub your face — with a dry towel — to take off all the impurities. Do this gently. You want to remove only the dirt, not your skin as well.

## Hair

Everybody's hair is different in lots of ways, in colour, in length, and in texture. Your hair may be greasy or dry, long or short, fine or wiry, curly or straight.

No matter what your hair is like, you should try to keep it as clean and in as good condition as possible. You will know yourself whether you need to wash it every two or three days, or once a week. You should wash your hair at least once every seven or eight days. You should wash it when it looks limp and greasy, when it separates and does not sit well when you comb it, or when your head starts to feel itchy. A regular family shampoo from the supermarket is suitable for most people. If your hair is very dry you may want to use a conditioner, perhaps once a week. Again you can buy these quite reasonably from the local supermarket. Some of the large chain stores produce shampoos and conditioners under their own name. These are usually cheaper, and are often very good indeed as they are made by well-known companies specially for certain stores. Do not be afraid to try out a few different products and change to another brand every now and again.

There are lots of different ways in which your hair can be damaged. You should have it cut or trimmed regularly to prevent 'split ends'. These are caused by the individual hairs splitting into two or even three strands. If you do not have these cut off, the split can go on up towards your scalp and spoil the texture and appearance of your hair. Next time you are outside, take a long piece of grass and split it into three strands to see what can happen to your hair.

Hair colour, perms and excessive use of hair spray, heated tongs or brushes can also damage your hair. Conditioners can help to a certain extent.

It is worthwhile finding a hairdresser you like and trust, and then going back to the same person. You only need to go once every two or three months to have the ends trimmed. Remember, you will find excellent hairdressers in your local area, in small shops, who do not charge exorbitant prices. You do not need to go to large upmarket salons. You should look for a good hairdresser, not plush surroundings.

# Hands and nails

Your hands are one of the few parts of your body which are constantly 'on show' to the world around you. Because you use your hands in most things you do, you have to pay attention to keeping them clean, so that you do not carry dirt and infection, keeping them efficient, so that they remain useful tools, and keeping them looking presentable so that people do not recoil in horror when they see them.

You should wash your hands thoroughly several times a day: when you get up in the morning, before meals, and after you have been to the toilet. If you have been doing something messy like working on your bike, or helping in the garden, you should wash your hands when you have finished. Do not think it is bad to get your hands dirty, just make sure you do not keep them that way.

If you are working with food, your hands need particular attention. Wash them before you begin to prepare food, and if you chop onions or garlic, or something with a strong smell, wash away the traces from your fingers so that you do not produce onion-flavoured rock cakes!

You should also clean your nails with a nailbrush once a day. Dirt can easily get lodged under your nails, and can look awful, as well as being a possible source of infection. You should cut your nails regularly, either with scissors or with nail clippers, or file them using a diamond-cut nail file. Files are not expensive to buy, and are better for your nails because they do not tear them. Watch not to cut or file into the side of your finger. You will know you have done this if the side of your finger beside the nail feels hot, begins to go red, or begins to swell. This may happen too if you bite down the side of your nail and tear out the cuticle. You can dip your finger very gently in hot water to try to stop the infection. Leave it for a couple of days, and if it becomes very sore, go and see your doctor, as you may have the beginnings of an infection, or an ingrown nail. If a little yellow pus develops at the side of your finger, do not pierce this with a needle or a pin, and do not squeeze it, as this will only make it worse.

Many people complain that their nails are soft and tear easily, or that they are brittle and break. Sometimes drinking more milk can help this, as the calcium in milk is good for nails (as well as teeth). Chemists sell commercially produced 'nail-hardeners', and these can be very effective. When you are looking after your nails, do not cut away the cuticles, or push them back with hard manicure tools or orange sticks. If you soak your hands in warm water for a few minutes, you will be able to gently tidy the cuticles by easing them back with the towel as you dry your hands.

Many teenagers bite their nails, nibble away the skin at the side of their fingers, or tear off the cuticles or top of the nails. There are lots of reasons why people do this — they may be anxious, tense or bored. If you bite your nails you may not even realise you are doing it. Look at your own nails. If you do bite them, try to think when and why you do it. Try to become conscious of when you put your fingers in your mouth.

Think about …

> … the risk of infection: you may be sucking your fingers just after you have touched money which has been lying around, or a door handle in the school (not the cleanest of objects!)
>
> … how you look with your fingers in your mouth
>
> … how unsightly your hands and nails are
>
> … how efficient your nails are as part of your working body: can you start to tear off a piece of sellotape with your nails, or do you have to use your teeth?

# Feet

Your feet are probably about 20 to 25 centimetres long, and yet they support your whole body which is about eight to ten times their own size. Most people use their feet whenever they move around, so it is important to look after them, to avoid sores and deformities even in your teens.

Janice is an attractive girl of 16, who really likes to keep up to date with her clothes. Luckily for her, the shoes she likes to wear give her toes plenty of room to spread as she walks, and are not so high that she throws her back out of line. Her brother is also very clothes-conscious. The shoes he chose to wear cramped his toes. He developed a pad of hard skin down the middle of the ball of his foot. The joint under his big toe became red and painful, and the doctor said he would probably have a severe bunion by the time he was twenty.

Your feet soon complain if you are wearing shoes which are bad for you or do not fit. Your heels or your little toes go red or become blistered. When you take your shoes off, you sigh with relief, and your feet swell up. The first thing you should do is throw away the shoes. If you do have blisters, or red patches, soak your feet in warm water, dry them thoroughly and then rub on some hand cream. Do not burst the blisters. When you put shoes on again, put talcum powder on your feet before you put your socks or tights on. Rubbing surgical spirit on your feet can help to toughen the skin without making it go hard, but do not do this if you have open blisters or sores on your feet. Wait until they are healed.

You should wash your feet every day if possible — it only takes five minutes. Wear clean socks or tights every day so that you do not carry around yesterday's sweat, and wear shoes that fit and are comfortable — they do not have to be old-fashioned or ugly.

# Eyes

Your eyes need looking after too. You wash round them as you wash your face, but you can also splash them with cold water to make them feel fresh. If you wake up in the morning to find a little crust on your eyelashes, do not worry, this will wash off easily and is quite normal. If your eyelids are stuck together, or if the crusty bits seem excessive, you may have a slight infection, and should see your doctor.

Your eyes are very delicate parts of your body and you must take care not to damage them by rubbing them or poking at them. If they are sore or itchy, your eyes are letting you know that there is something wrong. Do you strain your eyes by watching too much television with all the lights out, or by reading under the blankets with a torch?

As a check, you should have your eyes tested regularly by an optician. If you are short-sighted, long-sighted or have an astigmatism (when your eye is slightly out of shape) you may have to wear glasses. Some teenagers feel very self-conscious about wearing glasses, because they feel it makes them less attractive. However some frames can be very fashionable. You may want to consider contact lenses which often cost about the same as a pair of specs. Lenses, however, do need special soaking and cleaning solutions, which can be expensive. You have to make sure you know how much money is really involved.

## Ears

Your ears are a very complex part of your body, and are much more than just the bits that stick out on each side of your head. This outer ear only catches the sound so that it goes more easily to the inner ear which 'hears' it. Try putting your hands up behind your ears. You should find that your hear slightly better because you are creating bigger sound traps with your hands. You should try not to get too much water inside your ears, although washing round your ears (and behind them), and washing your hair will not do any damage.

Do not poke *anything* around inside your ears. Even cotton buds can do damage. You can also damage your inner ears by holding your nose when you sneeze, since the force of your sneeze goes up inside your ears. If your ears buzz or feel blocked, hold the end of your nose, and gently breathe down, then swallow hard. You may get this feeling in a long tunnel if you are on a train, or when you are in an aeroplane. If you hear ringing in your ears, or your ears feel blocked all the time, see your doctor.

# Teeth

Adults should have about 32 teeth, but many countries have high rates of tooth decay. This is caused by what we eat, for instance the amount of sugar, cakes and sweets we eat. You should brush your teeth every day, once in the morning and once before you go to bed. If you can manage it, you should brush your teeth after you have eaten, but this is not always possible. However, you can carry a toothbrush and a small tube of toothpaste in your pocket so that you can brush your teeth after you have had lunch in school, or been for a quick snack.

Most toothpastes now have fluoride added to them and this gives your teeth added protection. You can also buy 'disclosing' tablets, which you suck to show you where you have left plaque (a film of bacteria) on your teeth. They contain a harmless pink dye.

You should have a check-up at your dentist every six months, even if you think you do not need anything done. When you have no fillings to be done, the dentist may polish your teeth and scrape away tartar, which collects on and between your teeth. This 'scrape and polish' is painless and will help you keep your teeth in good order.

## A word to the girls ...

If you are a girl, you may decide to shave your legs or armpits to remove hair. You can do this simply by soaping your skin and lightly running a safety razor over it. Do not press too hard, as you may cut into your skin and make yourself bleed. You can also remove hair by using an electric razor, by using hair-removing cream, or by waxing. Do not do this yourself, as the wax has to be hot and you can easily burn yourself. Do not use hair-removing cream on your eyebrows — it can easily get into your eyes and cause damage. If you have hair on your face, or round your chin, which you do not like, do not use a razor, and do not pluck it as both will make the hair grow in even stronger. You are probably the only one to notice it.

You will need to pay particular attention to personal hygiene during your period, as you may perspire more than usual. Change your sanitary pad or tampon each time you go to the toilet. You should wrap the soiled pad in paper and put it in the bin — not down the toilet.

Remember that your vaginal area is a most delicate membrane. Never wash yourself with strong soap, or use vaginal deodorant. These can only irritate the skin or dry up normal fluids which are necessary for vaginal health. You may notice a slight trace of this fluid on your pants. This is quite normal and is nothing to worry about. If it becomes very heavy, or if it is brownish or greenish in colour, or if it smells nasty, or if you feel itchy, you should see your doctor, who will check that everything is all right.

## ... And to the boys

During puberty and adolescence both boys and girls experience many different changes in the way their bodies behave. Boys experience nocturnal emissions ('wet dreams'), when they ejaculate semen, often while they are still asleep. This is quite normal. Unlike female organs, male genital organs are outside the body but still need special care and attention. For example, you should not use strong soaps or deodorants round or on your genitals. If you notice any soreness when you urinate, or any discharge from the tip of your penis, you should go and see a doctor.

An important part of personal hygiene and growing up for boys is beginning to shave. Because your skin and your 'beard' are still quite soft, shaving can cause soreness and even spots. A gentle electric razor may help to avoid this, but if you do not have one, or would rather use a regular safety razor, lightly smear your face with a moisturising cream (one that does not have perfume in it) before putting on your shaving foam. This should prevent your skin breaking out in spots or becoming inflamed. Try to avoid aftershave lotions for a while as most of them contain alcohol which will only irritate any little sore patches.

## A final word

Using soap and water on various parts of your body is what personal hygiene is all about, but drying off that soap and water is just as important. Soap has a drying effect on skin, so you should make sure that there is none left on your skin to dry and irritate it. Water too can chafe and irritate skin if it gets trapped in folds such as between your toes and fingers, under your earlobes, or between your legs. You should make sure that all these places are dry, otherwise your skin may crack and break into little cuts. A shake of talcum powder can help make sure that your skin is dried off thoroughly.

# 5. Health at Risk

We all have our own ideas of what it means to be healthy. It can mean having the energy and interest to take part in lots of activities, being able to run a mile in under four minutes, being happy and nice to be with, or being attractive to other people. Think what health means to you and the people around you.

Illness too means lots of different things to different people, but most of us would agree that being ill means feeling unwell, having a germ or infection which attacks parts of our bodies, or suffering from problems caused by an accident or disease. There are activities which you may decide to take part in, in the full knowledge that there is a risk involved: for instance, if you decide you want to go skiing, you know there is a risk you may fall and break your leg. There are other problems with health that human beings can suffer, for instance allergies, infections and disease.

Most teenagers do not think about dying of a heart attack or a stroke. These do happen to teenagers, but only rarely, and it is difficult to imagine that you may one day in the future suffer from heart disease because it is so far away in time. There are problems and illnesses which teenagers do suffer from however, both in the 'risk' and in the second category. You should try to think what risk you take with your health.

Richard did a lot of BMX biking at weekends near the quarry behind the estate where he lived. One day his

26

pal Brian dared him to a game of 'chicken' to see who would stop first in a race to the edge of the quarry. Brian lost the game because he stopped first. Richard lost the use of his legs because he went over the edge and broke his back.

## Areas of risk

Many teenagers take risks by abusing their systems with tobacco or alcohol. Because the risks from these are long-term, and seem far away, it is very easy to say 'It won't happen to me'. This is wrong.

Solvent abuse, glue-sniffing and drug abuse, for example, can all cause major problems. Many young people have died in their early teens because they have

taken drugs or solvents. Some have committed suicide, and some have died because their bodies could no longer cope with the poison being pumped into them. There are no set reasons why young people take drugs or sniff glue. If you have already tried these, you have been taking serious risks with your health and wellbeing.

Some areas of risk, however, are more difficult to sort out, because there is a good side and a bad side. Sexual activity is just one of these. Having a relationship with someone, being in love, being close and intimate with another person is one of the greatest feelings in the world. But sexual activity brings with it the risk of sexually transmitted disease such as herpes and gonorrhea, which both boys and girls can catch. Boys usually notice the symptoms much quicker than girls; because female reproductive organs are inside, girls may have gonorrhoea and not even know it. If you notice any discharge or soreness in your genitals, and if you know that you have had intercourse or heavy petting with someone you do not know very well, you should contact your doctor. If you do not want to go and see your own family doctor, go into your local hospital where there will be a 'special' clinic. It is in the telephone book under 'VD Advice'.

Every year many teenage girls of 15, 14 and even 13 become pregnant. The majority of these do not want the baby, and decide to to have an abortion, or have the baby adopted. Whatever happens, girls feel the effects of pregnancy for a long time — mentally and physically.

Annie was in third year at school and was studying hard for her exams. She had been going out with Mike for nearly eight months and really loved him. One evening, they were babysitting for Annie's sister. They had poured a couple of glasses of wine, and were petting heavily. They both said they loved each other and did not feel it was wrong to have sex. It was the first time for both of them. Annie got pregnant.

They both had to cope with their parents' confusion, worry and anger over what had happened. They had to try to make a decision about whether Annie should have an abortion, but they both knew the serious risks involved in that. Both of them ended up very confused and unhappy. There are no happy endings to stories like this.

Having a sexual relationship with another person is a responsibility which can bring a great deal of pleasure, but part of that responsibility is not taking risks with the health or welfare of your partner. Contraception is not the girl's responsibility — both partners should decide what is best for them as a couple. Family Planning Centres have young people's clinics every week, and the Brook Advisory Service is specially for young people. Your parents and your family doctor are there too to help you make a decision about whether you want to be part of such a close relationship at this point.

## Prevention is better than cure

You do not decide to have a cold or flu in the same way that you decide to take a risk. There are many minor illnesses and problems that you can cope with and recover from. There are even some that you can prevent.

## Foot problems

It is very easy to pick up foot infections in places where people walk around in their bare feet, such as school showers, swimming pools and sports centre changing rooms. One of the most common is athlete's foot, when the skin between your toes becomes infected and sore, and then the skin on your foot becomes itchy and covered with a rash. Another common problem is having a verruca on the sole of your foot. This is a small wart-like growth which is easily spotted on the ball of your foot. If you think you have either of these, go to your doctor and he or she will give you an ointment to clear it up. Do not swim if you have either of these infections, use your own towel, and if you do any exercise, wear your own socks, and wear plastic shoes in the shower.

You should keep your toenails short, but always cut them after you have soaked them in a basin or a bath as they will be softer then and will cut easily. If toenails are not cut properly you can develop an ingrown toenail, where the nail begins to grow into the side of your toe. This can be very painful, and quite difficult to get rid of. You should go and see your doctor if you have any soreness, tenderness or redness at the side of your toenails.

Chilblains are common in the winter, and you can get these on your fingers or on your toes. Your skin becomes red and itchy, but if you scratch the itchy areas your skin breaks and gets very sore. If you do have itchy fingers or toes and you think it may be due to the cold, dab on a little tincture of iodine (the brown stuff is best) as long as your skin is not broken. This takes away the itch and can help clear the problem up. If it gets too bad, you should go to your doctor.

## 'Girls' troubles'

Many teenage girls suffer cramps and pain during their periods. Exercise can help, but if they get too bad you can ease the pain slightly by getting a simple pain-killer from the chemist. Sitting down or lying with a hot-water bottle against your stomach may also help. If you do lie down, stretch yourself out gently and watch not to pull any of your tummy muscles too suddenly. If you have to stay off school because of period pains, you should see your doctor.

Many people think that thrush and cystitis (pronounced sist-eye-tis) are female problems. They are most common in girls and women, but boys and men can suffer from them too.

In girls, the vagina has normal bacteria which live there and keep infections away. Sometimes, though, bacteria called yeast bacteria take over, causing thrush, and you may feel itchy and sore, because the bacteria are out of balance. This can happen if you wear tight clothing such as jeans, and sometimes if you wear nylon underwear, which can make you too hot. Cotton underwear and loose clothing can prevent thrush. If you do feel a slight itch, dab on some natural yoghurt, which will help take away the itch, cool you down and help the normal vaginal bacteria grow again. A word of warning — some antibiotics can cause thrush as a side effect. Always tell the doctor if this has happened to you before.

Cystitis is a urinary-tract infection — when the urinary passage becomes infected. You feel that you need to go to the toilet every five or so minutes, and feel a burning sensation and pain if you do pass water. If you feel this coming on, drink lots of warm water, or tea and coffee, and see a doctor as soon as possible. You can help prevent cystitis by washing regularly, and wiping your bottom from 'front to back' when you go to the toilet.

## Allergies

Many people are allergic to everyday things. You may have found out already that you are sensitive or allergic to dogs or cats, or fur coats and feather pillows. If you are allergic to something you may sneeze a lot, your eyes may swell up, or you may develop a rash or red lumps when you are in contact with your own particular problem. Some people are allergic to dairy products, and there is now lots of evidence to suggest that many of the additives in food cause anxiety or nervousness in some children and young people. If you do have an allergy, always tell your doctor, as this may effect his choice of medicine for you for other problems.

You may be sensitive to soaps, soap powders or even perfume or talc. If you do develop a rash for no reason, check to see whether you have changed your soap recently.

If your allergy makes you sneeze, you will always find people who find it annoying, because they think you have a cold. They do not understand or sympathise and often think you are acting up or tell you that 'it's all in the mind!'

Allergies are very real problems however and you should avoid any source of your particular allergy

whenever you can. Your doctor can help too with medicine to relieve the symptoms.

## Good health

Doctors, along with all the other nursing and care services, are there to help you if you do become ill. You should find out about the people who are there to help you in the departments of health, education and social services.

Your health however is *your* responsibility. You can do certain things, like watching your diet, taking exercise, and maintaining different parts of your body, which will all help you stay healthy. On the other hand you may do things like smoking, abusing solvents or not eating properly, which will harm you.

You have to choose what you do to your body.

# 6. Sharing Health

Every day people share their germs, their colds and flu with others around them, by sneezing and coughing. More serious illnesses like typhoid, herpes and dysentery can be shared just as easily.

Health means being positive rather than negative. You can promote health by sharing your health, just as you tend to share your illnesses.

Keeping yourself clean, and free from infections like athlete's foot, and taking responsibility for sexual activity all mean that you promote not only your own health, but that of your friends and families as well.

There are other practical ways too of sharing your health. You can share your energy by washing the dishes or hoovering the carpet when your parents are tired and could do with help. You can share your feelings by being civil to people around you instead of being grumpy. They will treat you better too, and you will feel the benefits in turn. You can share your sympathy by trying to help those who need a hand now and again. You can share the fact that you are growing into an adult by thinking before you snap at somebody for no good reason. Remember — it is very important that you learn to share your health with others so that it becomes a nice habit for the rest of your life.

# 7. Healthy Through and Through

Health is not just about not being ill, nor is it just about being physically fit and well, keeping clean, and eating the right things. All these are important, and help make you the person you are, but you should try to decide what other aspects of life you think are important for your health.

Lisa is 15, pretty, shy and intelligent. She works hard at school and cycles home to the farm where she lives with her family. At nights, she does her homework and watches television. At the weekends she helps on the farm, where she looks after the hens. Other girls in her class at school have asked her to meet them at the weekend, but she has always said she is too busy. They did not realise that she was so shy that she felt quite frightened and nervous about going out with them. In the end they gave up asking. Even at school now Lisa is on her own. She feels very lonely. She wishes that only one of the girls would ask her to go out, just the two of them. Then she could pluck up the courage to go out with all the others, as a group.

Getting on well with other people and being a person in your own right are part of being healthy too.

## Getting to know yourself

Growing up and becoming an adult is a difficult time. As well as changing physically, you are changing mentally and emotionally and you begin to develop sexual feelings. Adolescence is a time of change — from a child to an adult.

Different countries have different laws about the age at which you are allowed to do 'adult' things. For instance, at 16 in Scotland, and 18 in England and Wales, you can get married without your parents' permission. At 17 you can sit your driving test, at 18 you can vote, take out a hire-purchase agreement and be called up if there is a war. But growing up is not just something to do with the law.

During adolescence you will encounter many important milestones in your life and you have to consider how you can cope with them. One of the best ways to face all these changes is to try to get to know yourself a bit better. We all have different characteristics. You should make a list of the things that you know about yourself.

You will probably not like everything about yourself, and you may think that some of your own characteristics are bad. But you are probably not as bad as you think — everyone has some good points. Take a piece of paper, put the date on it, and write down all the good and bad things about yourself. Nobody else will see what you write, so you should try to be as honest as you can.

What you have written down will tell you what your 'self-image' is — or what and how you think of yourself. Write down words which describe you physically and the way you act as a person. There should be a balance of both. Do this again in six months' time and compare the two to see what differences there are.

Try to begin to recognise how you act in certain circumstances. Did you really need to wallop your little brother when he annoyed you? Did you really need to sulk when you were scolded for hitting him? Part of being grown-up is being able to act the way you decide to act. So you are in control of what you do.

## As others see you

The famous Scots poet Robert Burns wrote words to the effect that it would be great if we could see ourselves as others see us. In trying to work out what you think are your good and bad points, listen to what other people say to you, listen when they tell you that you have done something well — it may happen more often than you think.

One way that you can see yourself as others see you is by looking in the mirror. Clothes can say a lot about you, which is why they are so important. Young people who wear punk clothes and do their hair in unconventional ways are trying to tell the world how they feel — and they have the right to do so. Similarly if you wear a collar and tie or a smart dress when you go

for a job interview you are saying that you are willing to fit in, and this is just as right. Your clothes say something about you. Do they make an accurate statement to the world?

## Getting to know other people

Other people help us decide how we act. It is important for our health to be sociable and to be able to get on well with other people. You do not have to be the life and soul of the party if that is not the sort of person you are, but by being yourself with your family and friends, by enjoying the characteristics you like about yourself, you build your self-confidence and self-esteem.

## Powerful persuaders

As you grow up and mix with other people, you will find that some of them will try to make you do what they want you to do, even though you may not want to. Your friends may try to get you to smoke, drink or sniff glue. 'Go on, baby — too frightened to try it?' 'Worried about what mummy will say if she catches you?'

You may feel confused too about the messages you hear about sex. Your parents may be telling you not to have sex, but on television all the good guys and successful girls sleep together without a thought. There are lots of myths and old wives' tales too which are wrong and should be ignored. Some people think that if you have sex standing up the girl will not get pregnant. This is not true. Some people will tell you that masturbating gives you spots, or makes you go blind ... or deaf ... or mad. This is also not true. Masturbating is quite normal, will give you pleasure and will not harm you.

Remember it is not just girls who feel confused. Boys may try to persuade their girlfriends to have sex by saying 'You would if you loved me', but girls have sexual feelings too and may encourage the boy by saying 'Do you not love me enough?'

Boys can be hurt as easily as girls if someone they care for lets them down. You have to decide for yourself what you want from a relationship, and what you are prepared to give. If you want to have sex, you should think about what your relationship means to you. You should consider how you know when you can trust someone. How can you be sure that somebody really cares for you, and that they won't hurt you?

Taking part in a sexual and loving relationship is a big commitment. It cannot be covered here. You should talk to people you trust and read other books to help you decide how you feel.

Young people are an important group for advertisers on television and in newspapers and magazines. You will recognise adverts that are specially aimed at people like yourself. But not all young people want to buy the same things, or look the same — you have to stand up for your own opinions.

# 8. Good Health

Health is about physical, mental and social wellbeing. It is about your self-image and self-confidence; you should feel good about the way you feel, look and act. You have to decide for yourself how you are going to live and how healthy you are going to be. It is up to you. You are in charge.